HAND TIED BOUQUETS

Aad van Uffelen
Translation Tom Colin

TERRA

CONTENTS

The spiral or sheaf technique is the most used binding technique used today. This bouquet contains 200 stems and is finished with a beautiful bow. It is free standing in a handcrafted Mobach pottery bowl surrounded with pebbles and sand.

Front cover:
The sheaf or spiral binding technique is used in this all round hand tied bouquet. The bouquet consists of the following materials: *Salvia nemorosa, Centaurea cyanus, Aconitum, Ageratum, Campanula glomerata, Centaurea montana, Eustoma, Phlox, Rosa* 'Larinii', *Scabiosa, Trachelium, Triteleia, Veronica, Hydrangea, Clematis, Lupinus, Campanula latifolia, Eryngium planum, Eryngium alpinum, Spiraea bumalda, Erigeron, Bupleurum griffithii, Deutzia, Thuja, Euonymus.*

Back cover:
• *(above)*
The sheaf or spiral binding technique is used in this all round bouquet. Used are the following materials: *Ranunculus, Gysophila, Allium moly, Arachniodes adiantiformis, Asparagus setaceus.*
• *(below)*
Binding technique is the sheaf or parallel. Flowers used are: *Dendranthema, Lilium, Dianthus caryophyllus, Limonium, Ammi majus, Hypericum, Asparagus virgatus, Ruscus, Arachniodes adiantiformis, Taxus baccata* 'Fastigiata'.

FOREWORD

Although the dimension of this book may seem rather small, it does, however, contain a wealth of information as well as a wide range of techniques and bouquet styles.
The study of simple basic techniques, which may lead to original and varied new techniques, is the purpose and thread which runs through this informative book.
It is not at all difficult to create or reproduce attractive and original bouquets.
The reason for this book is to help you get started and explain the techniques, backgrounds and other pertinent information, including many examples to create beautiful bouquets.
Bouquet making is extremely popular and rather fun to do.
I wish you much enjoyment in reading this book, but even more so in making attractive and exciting hand tied bouquets.

Naaldwijk, Spring 1997

Aad van Uffelen

BOUQUETS BRING ATMOSPHERE

The hand tied bouquet is one of the most attractive forms of flower arranging. It is really not that difficult, nor does it take much time to make a charming little bouquet. Gather a few flowers and foliage in the hand and tie them with a little piece of string. A vase filled with water to which the correct amount of flower food has been added, will ensure a long lasting bouquet.

Hand tied bouquets belong to the oldest and most important forms of flower arranging, and enjoy popularity worldwide.

There are many reasons for making a hand tied bouquet, but in whatever form they are presented, they are always well received.

Trend bouquets, such as the cascade style, the romantic style bouquet, and bouquets which include ribbons, pieces of fabric, bullion, copper wire, spice sticks, including bouquets which feature binding construction as a basis of design, are always enjoyable to make and project your individual creativity.

There is much confusion regarding terminology. In order to clarify the situation, we shall speak of only hand tied and wired bouquets. A flower arrangement is not classified as a bouquet, however, a little problem arises, because a bridal bouquet arranged in a bouquet holder, filled with floral foam, is also called a bouquet. At present, many bouquets are made using a combination of wiring and gluing techniques, therefore, definitions of bouquet terminology are not always clear cut.

There are many ways to make attractive and creative bouquets. This book will try to assist you by demonstrating various techniques in hand tying bouquets, using many colour combinations, appropriately finished with ribbon, foliage and/or foil. When presented with flair, they become irresistible as gifts or to be enjoyed in one's home.

TOOLS

One does not need many tools to make a bouquet. A simple kitchen knife will cut most flower stems, with the exception of thick branches. The flower stems need to be cut on a 45 degree angle for best results. A pair of sharp pruning shears is best to cut through thick branches or stems. When your bouquet is finished, cut all stems straight across. Use wire cutters in case you want to wire the flowers in your bouquet.

TECHNIQUES

There are a variety of ways to create a bouquet in the hand. The result varies depending on the chosen techniques. The following elements play a role in the construction of a bouquet:

a. The choice of materials, combination, form and colour.
b. The preparation of the materials; the attachment of flowers, foliage, fruits, moss, cushion of straw etc. to florist wire or wired wooden picks, when needed.
c. The use of floral tape or para film.
d. The tying of individual groups or components.
e. The application of ribbon, foil, paper, crepe paper.
f. The binding and tying materials, e.g. string, raffia, ribbon, floral tape, wire, elastics.
g. Glue to fasten components in the bouquet.
h. The tying, binding points and tying techniques.
i. The finishing touches, final cutting.
j. Packaging and decorative touches.

Plan the bouquet making activity carefully and prepare the necessary materials. Remove the lower leaves from the flower stems and have the tying material at hand, including the necessary tools. Prevent damage to flowers and foliage by placing them in pails of water, or lay them carefully on the table, sorted as to variety and colour. Limit the use of florist wire as this can cause unsightly rust stains in pottery or glass vases. If desired, florist wire may be covered with floral tape.

Tying techniques
One can choose from a variety of techniques to assemble a bouquet. The most common is the spiral or sheaf technique, in which the flowers are bound in a spiral form.

There is also the parallel technique in which the stems are placed in a straight line, side by side.

Still other alternative techniques are available, which include the combination of wired and gluing techniques, weaving techniques and the base or grid construction through which the flowers are placed. The technique in which the flowers are assembled in a criss cross fashion is not recommended as it does not result in a pleasing looking bouquet.

Sheaf or spiral technique
A. This is the standard assembly technique used in making a round bouquet. (The following explanation is for right-handed people; left-handed people should do the reverse).
a. Take some foliage or evergreen branches in the left hand and place the principal flower in the centre (sketch 1).
b. All materials to the left of the centre flower are placed diagonally in front (sketch 2 and 3).
c. All materials to the right of the centre flower are placed diagonally behind (sketch 4).
d. Continue to assemble the bouquet in this fashion by adding flowers to the left and right as described above, making sure that the stems conform to the spiral technique. If some of the stems are crossed or misplaced, pull out and re-insert. It is advisable to turn the bouquet regularly while adding flowers to ensure an attractive and uniform round shape.
e. Add foliage to provide a finishing touch, and check final form.

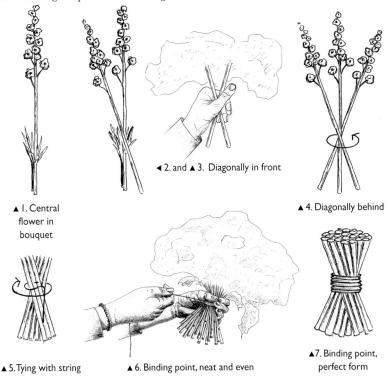

▲ 1. Central flower in bouquet

◄ 2. and ▲ 3. Diagonally in front

▲ 4. Diagonally behind

▲ 5. Tying with string

▲ 6. Binding point, neat and even

▲ 7. Binding point, perfect form

f. Tie the bouquet firmly, but not too tightly to avoid crushing or cutting the stems (sketch 5, 6 and 7). Tie the string neatly around the base of the bouquet and pull the string carefully upward through the stems. This method will lock the string in place. Some people, however, prefer tying both ends of the string together.

g. Ribbon, raffia, etc. may be used to provide an extra festive touch.

B. An alternative *spiral technique* which provides excellent results, especially when making large bouquets is as follows:

a. Take some foliage or evergreen branches in the left hand (left-handed people use right hand) and place principal flower in the centre.

b. Place all flowers crosswise in front till sufficient flowers have been added to form a nice shape.

c. Turn bouquet 180 degrees using both hands and add flowers to the other side as explained in step b. The result will be an attractive bouquet.

Parallel technique, stems side by side

Parallel technique

With this technique all stems are placed side by side in a straight line. Flowers thus used will make the bundle of flower stems rather slim, and therefore ideally suited for bridal or presentation bouquets. Linear styled bouquets benefit from using the parallel binding technique as well. For large bouquets it is advisable to make individual groups or bundles of the tallest flowers. This makes the assembly of the bouquet easier as it prevents the shifting or movement of individual flowers. The tying of this bouquet occurs in two places; the first by tying individual components together as we tie the bouquet, the second as a finishing technique under the last leaves.

Alternative techniques

Combination and new techniques have been introduced into the realm of hand tied bouquets. The most attractive and innovative of these techniques is the construction of a basis structure, e.g. sphere, ring or grid made from *Salix* (willow), *Cornus* (dogwood) or other pliable branches. Flowers are placed and supported between these branches or structures and tied in the usual manner.

Combination techniques are used when various components such as moss, shells, etc. are to be included in the bouquet. These items are fastened to florist wire and included in the so-called 'structure' bouquets.

The above mentioned techniques will be further explained as part of the descriptions of the example bouquets.

TIP: WHEN YOUR BOUQUET IS ALMOST FINISHED, BUT YOU FEEL THAT CERTAIN FLOWERS ARE NOT QUITE IN THE RIGHT PLACE, PULL THEM OUT AND REPOSITION THEM, MAKING SURE THAT THE STEMS FOLLOW THE SAME DIRECTION AS THE STEMS IN THE BOUQUET.

TIP: IF SOFT STEMMED FLOWERS ARE USED IN THE BOUQUET, PLACE SOME EVERGREEN OR OTHER FOLIAGE AROUND THEM TO PREVENT THE STEMS FROM BEING CRUSHED OR CUT BY THE BINDING CORD/STRING.

TIP: LARGE BOUQUETS MAY BE ASSEMBLED AND TIED IN STAGES WITH FRESH FLORAL MATERIALS ADDED AS NEEDED OR TIME PERMITS.

TIP: GROUP AND TIE SMALL BUNCHES OF FLOWERS TOGETHER BEFORE ASSEMBLING THEM INTO A LARGER BOUQUET. FLOWERS THUS ARRANGED WILL STAY WHERE THEY ARE PLACED.

TIP: A SIMPLE WAY TO CREATE A ONE SIDED BOUQUET, ESPECIALLY WHEN LARGE, IS TO LAY THE FLOWERS CAREFULLY ON THE TABLE, WHILE HOLDING THE FLOWER STEMS IN THE HAND.
ADD MORE FLOWERS TO THE BOUQUET UNTIL YOU ARE SATISFIED WITH THE RESULTS.

ACCESSORIES

a. Bow on a stick
b. Cushion of hay on a stick
c. Fruit on a stick

Accessories are materials which facilitate the making of hand tied bouquets. Binding materials, such as string, raffia, curling ribbon, florist wire, spool wire, glue and floral tape are all used to tie or hold the bouquet together.
Of all these, string is the most popular means of tying a bouquet, but raffia, curling ribbon and floral tape are a close second.
Very large bouquets are often bound with strong waterproof tape to secure the stems.
Bamboo canes or slender twigs (sketch 3) are frequently used to tie on ribbons, foil, cushions of moss or hay and fruit, and can thus easily be inserted into the bouquet.

Wire is frequently used to strengthen and support flowers and foliage, and has the ability to bend and shape the flower stems into the desired direction or form. It is important to use the correct gauge (thickness) of wire. Use the lightest (thinnest) gauge possible to support the flowers.
Hollow stemmed flowers can be invisibly supported by inserting a heavy gauge wire into the stem.
When flowers or foliage need to be shaped to create special effects, place a heavy gauge wire alongside the stem and cover with floral tape. You are now able to carefully shape the stem without breaking. This technique works well with flowers and foliage, which have flexible stems such as *Allium*, *Gerbera*, *Ruscus*, etc.
An alternative method is to let the flower wilt, so the soft stem can then be wired and shaped easily. After wiring and shaping, recut the flower on a slant and place in water to become fully turgid; only then can it be used in the bouquet.
The gluing technique is quite often used to glue various materials in the bouquet such as seed pods and other non living components. Sometimes fresh flowers are glued for use in bouquets; especially bridal bouquets benefit from this technique. Flowers which have been glued will last somewhat longer if they have been sprayed with 'Clear Life' or similar spray to retard evaporation.
Flowers, of course, last longest when placed in water and flower food.

CHOICE OF MATERIALS

The challenge is to choose compatible materials which will lead to the creation of a beautiful bouquet. We are talking here about the choice of a large variety of flowers with respect to form, structure, texture and contrast. Colour, of course, plays a dominant role. Green and grey coloured foliage not only create resting points in a bouquet, but also heighten the effects of structure and contrast.
Choose materials of a similar lasting quality. Use well developed foliage and flowers which have been cut at the right stage of development.
Young light green foliage and flowers in tight buds will not open and wilt prematurely.
Correct material selection means the choosing of the right flowers, the right foliage, compatible accessories and appropriate attributes, such as berries, etc.
All of these choices should lead to the creation of a harmonious and exciting bouquet to suit the occasion.
It is advisable to familiarize oneself with the attributes and characteristics of the flowers, such as lasting quality, toxicity, fragrance, staining, such as the pollen of lilies.

One should not only create beautiful bouquets, but also user friendly bouquets, for example, by removing the stamen of lilies and the thorns of roses.
Many of the flowers used in this book are commercially available.

> TIP: ENVIRONMENTALLY FRIENDLY BOUQUETS.
> TRENDS ARE DEVELOPING, ESPECIALLY IN THE NETHERLANDS WITH RESPECT TO GROWING FLOWERS IN AN ECOLOGICALLY RESPONSIBLE WAY, WITHOUT THE USE OF PESTICIDES, FUNGICIDES AND IN AN ENERGY EFFICIENT MANNER.
> VARIOUS ASSOCIATIONS HAVE BEEN FORMED TO ADVISE AND ENSURE THAT SPECIFIC STANDARDS ARE ADHERED TO, SO THAT GROWERS MAY USE AND DISPLAY THE 'ENVIRO FRIENDLY SEAL' ON THEIR FLORAL PRODUCTS.
> WHEN USING THESE FLOWERS USE ONLY NATURAL TYING MATERIALS, SUCH AS UNBLEACHED STRING OR RAFFIA TO REINFORCE THE ENVIRONMENTAL NATURE OF THE BOUQUET. FIELD FLOWERS FALL INTO THE ABOVE CATEGORY.

ATTRIBUTES AND ACCESSORIES

An attribute is a decorative object in a bouquet. An object represents something specific such as a heart shaped novelty in a Saint Valentine's bouquet or a Santa Claus figurine during the Christmas' season. Attributes can in fact express feelings and emotions in a bouquet whether it be a fantasy or a gift.

Accessories are materials which assist and enhance the decorative effects of a bouquet, such as ribbon, string, cord, decorative wool, feathers, florist foil, crepe paper, etc. They also determine the end result, and the atmosphere the bouquet will project.

COLOUR COMBINATIONS

Colour is indeed challenging and catches the eye instantly. The study of colour is a wide and sometimes confusing field. Therefore, it is wise to pay some attention pertaining to the choice and combination of colours for our bouquets. There are many options in this regard. Tastes differ and it is almost impossible to lay down absolute rules. Make use of your own intuition and colour sense.
Even so, a basic knowledge of existing colour theory in all aspects is useful.
The radiance a bouquet projects is almost always due to a well thought out colour scheme.
Colours, which are harmonious and are in tune with each other and their surroundings, are easy to live with. There are, of course, subjective influences regarding the use of colour; most of it has to do with personal preferences.
In choosing colour, we need to review some basic colour theories.
The dimensions of colour are hue, value and chroma. Hue refers to one colour as distinct from another, e.g. yellow as distinct from red, or blue and pink. These hues come together in a bouquet, projecting specific emotions, such as excitement, quiet elegance, brilliance or reflection.
Colour symbolism can provide an extra dimension in a bouquet as well. Personal feelings, as well as the choice of colour and tonal values, play a large role in the making of a bouquet. Bright colours are often regarded as positive, while dull colours are experienced as negative. This, of course, depends on the country where one resides, and cultural influences.
To combine flowers effectively, use colour in the right proportion. A chart has been developed to make the selection easier, as it indicates the proportion of the various colours to be used. The chart assumes colours are of the same intensity.

Yellow	Orange	Red	Green	Blue	Violet
3	4	6	6	8	9

If a colour is stronger or weaker in intensity, use less or more of that same colour. Tension in a bouquet can be created when for example, a large area of yellow features a small speck of blue. This combination creates a dramatic dimension and evokes a specific radiation. The proportion of colour intensity between two or more colours is called contrast, often referred to as the difference between light and dark.
Colour contrasts form the basis of our choice of materials. We refer to the following theories for further clarification.
a. Chroma is contrasts between saturated colours, e.g. yellow, red, blue.
b. Value is contrasts between light and dark, e.g. yellow versus blue.
c. Cool and warm contrasts, e.g. orange and blue green.
d. Complementary contrasts, e.g. red and green.
e. Colour saturation contrasts, e.g. between light and dull colours.
f. Colour area contrasts between areas of colour of different formats.
Tone on tone has been for many years a favourite colour combination in the art of bouquet making. It is a monochromatic colour harmony which uses the tints, tones and shades of a colour, such as yellow to yellow orange.
Strong textural contrasts as well as extremes in values and chroma are all helpful in giving the bouquet a great deal of interest. Let your sense of colour and harmony be your guide.
It should be clear, that, without a proper colour choice we are not able to create a bouquet of distinction. Fortunately, most of us can rely on our innate sense of colour and guided by our intuition.

COMPOSITION AND FORM DEVELOPMENT

Form, like colour, immediately calls for attention. It is the hallmark of a successful bouquet. It can be constructed as a one sided or an all round bouquet; even a two sided bouquet arranged like a fan are some of the options available. The flowers and foliage can be mixed qua form or colour, or they could be grouped.
Grouping allows for rest points in a composition and is essential in a linear styled bouquet. The form can be symmetrical or asymmetrical. Within these forms one can arrange in a compact, open or linear pattern.
Unusual effects can be achieved by combining a diverse variety of materials in a criss cross and haphazard fashion, giving the appearance of an entangled, intertwined bouquet. We will discuss this form of arranging later in the book.
It is important that while arranging, the flowers are reasonably well distributed throughout the bouquet. The distribution of the materials can be divided in an even pattern, or in a more spontaneous and irregular fashion.
Structure is an often used word, but not always well understood in floral design. In terms of a bouquet, it is the total form and appearance in which it is constructed. Flowers, foliage and other materials possess their own texture, e.g. surface quality, such as: smooth, rough, coarse, fuzzy, etc. All materials arranged in a bouquet will, therefore, vie for attention.

FINISHING TOUCHES AND PACKAGING OF THE BOUQUET

Finishing touches
Bouquet stems can be finished with a great variety of materials, depending on availability and choice.
A very natural look is created by using palm fibre or large leaves from, for example, *Hosta, Bergenia*, etc. The above should be tied with natural binding materials such as string or raffia.
Another method is to use a single plastic cache pot. Fasten the pot with wire or cord. If wire is used, leave the ends long and bend

Wet tissue around bouquet stems in plastic bag

them upward into the bouquet between the stems to avoid injury. Ribbon, crepe paper and foil are all excellent choices, each displaying their own characteristics. Crepe paper is especially nice to use through the bouquet as well as a finishing touch around the stems. Unfortunately, it is not waterproof. It is advisable to tie a plastic bag around the stems before attaching the crepe paper collar.

When a bouquet is presented, it is important that the stems are dry and free from

A bouquet, packaged in contemporary materials, projects an entirely different image. Kraft paper and raffia are perceived as natural looking materials, and hence very popular.

thorns and wire (sketch 4). A plastic bag lined with wet tissue will greatly enhance the longevity of the bouquet. Fasten plastic bags before applying decorative finishes.

Small bouquets, often called 'Cradle Bouquets' in Europe, will greatly benefit from the above treatment.

Packaging. creating gifts of beauty

To make a bouquet is one thing, to create a beautiful gift is another. One can do this by using wrappings, for example, foil and paper, while ribbon, raffia and other decorative materials provide a festive touch. Make sure that the finishing touches complement, or contrast with the bouquet. Luxurious packaging provides extra value and makes the bouquet an 'exclusive' gift. It is advisable to wrap the bouquet during hot and cold weather conditions. Packaging, which

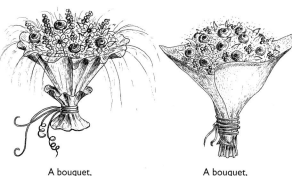

A bouquet, packaged in crepe paper

A bouquet, packaged in kraft paper

covers the lower half of the bouquet can be quite effective and could act as a decorative feature which can be placed with the bouquet into a vase. Transparent wrapping like cellophane enhances the visibility of a bouquet; however, it loses the surprise element as a gift. Wrap the bouquet lightly so as not to crush and damage the flowers.

TIP: A NOVELTY TOUCH IS TO WRAP THE BOUQUET IN THE PAGES OF A FLOWER OR GARDENING MAGAZINE. TAPE OR STAPLE SEVERAL PAGES TOGETHER. ALSO, LEFTOVER SHEETS OF WALLPAPER OR RE-CYCLED CRAFT PAPER, AND PACKAGING MATERIALS MAKE UNIQUE STATEMENTS.

TIP: SINGLE SHEETS OF PAPER OR FOIL ARE AVAILABLE AT CERTAIN SPECIALTY STORES.

CARE AND HANDLING OF FLOWERS IN THE BOUQUET

The flowers we use for making bouquets should be treated first before we arrange them. Even flowers bought from the florist should drink sufficient water before being used.

If you pick flowers from the garden directly, and arrange them in bouquets, they tend to wilt very quickly. Pick, therefore, flowers early in the morning when they are full of water (turgid).

Put flower food, such as 'Chrysal' in the water. This product prevents the formation of bacteria in the water, feeds the flowers and increases water uptake through the stem.

Care and preparation of the flowers
◆ Fill a container with tap water, 10 - 15 cm (sketch 7).
◆ Add flower food, the right kind and in exact proportion.
◆ Remove foliage from the lower end of the stem, approximately 1/3.
◆ Remove damaged and excessive foliage, including new shoots.
◆ Look at the flower and remove damaged petals.
◆ Cut flower stems with a sharp knife on a 45 degree angle.
◆ Place cut stems immediately in water.
◆ Let flowers drink at least 3 hours before arranging.
◆ During extreme heat or dryness, spray flowers overhead. This technique is not advisable for all flowers. An alternative technique is to drape a plastic sheet or bag like a tent over the pails of flowers to increase the level of humidity and retard evaporation.

Flower stem cut on a 45 degree angle

Certain flowers require special treatment
◆ *Bouvardia* and Chrysanthemums (*Dendranthema*) prefer to stand in cold water.
◆ Sunflowers, shrubs and flowers with woody stems require lukewarm water, which facilitates water absorption.
◆ Flower stems, which exude a white milky substance (Latex) such as *Euphorbia's* should be cut and placed in water till the running of sap has stopped (coagulated), remove from container and place in fresh water (sap is poisonous).

Do not torture flowers by burning the stem, putting stems in boiling water, splitting them, flattening the stems with a hard object or by breaking them. Cutting flowers with shears is not recommended, however, when necessary, one should use a pair of sharp pruning shears. Cutting flowers on a 45 degree angle with a sharp knife is still the best and preferred method.

TIP: WHEN FLOWERS SHOW SIGNS OF WILTING, WRAP THEM IN NEWSPAPER, CUT ENDS OF STEMS, PUT THEM IN WATER, AND PLACE IN A COOL LOCATION. LET STAND FOR APPROXIMATELY 3 HOURS BEFORE ARRANGING.

Care and handling of the bouquet
- Place bouquet away from sunlight, drafts, radiators and fresh fruit. Even smoke is detrimental for flowers.
- Top up vase daily with a flower food solution e.g. Chrysal.
- Remove spent blossoms in the bouquet.

Three kinds of flower food for long lasting bouquets:
- Chrysal Universal. Food for all fresh flowers, whether arranged in bouquets or flower arrangements.
- Chrysal Daffodil, which neutralizes the poisonous sap that is secreted by Daffodils and which is fatal for tulips and other fresh flowers.
- Chrysal Select is especially developed for bulb flowers and cut branch material, such as *Forsythia*, *Lilacs*, etc.

Beside Chrysal, there are numerous other flower care products, such as Floralife, etc. Florists use Chrysal Professional (trade name) to ensure long lasting flowers for their customers.

TIP: CLEAN VASES ARE ESSENTIAL FOR LONG LASTING FLOWERS. USE CLEANING AGENTS WHICH DO NOT CONTAIN CHLORINE AS THIS PRODUCT IS HARMFUL TO THE ENVIRONMENT. CHRYSAL CLEANER OR SIMILAR PRODUCT IS AN ENVIROMENTELLY SOUND ALTERNATIVE.

TIP: PLACE THE BOUQUET WITH OR NEAR SOME OF YOUR FAVOURITE ATTRIBUTES, OR DRAPE A ROMANTIC SCARF AROUND THE VASE.

PERIOD BOUQUETS

Research in the history of flowers and flower paintings provides us with some clues regarding the fashions in flower decoration and sometimes provides hints as to their construction and arrangement.
Period arrangements interpret the style and atmosphere of a particular historic period or artistic style. A brief synopsis follows:

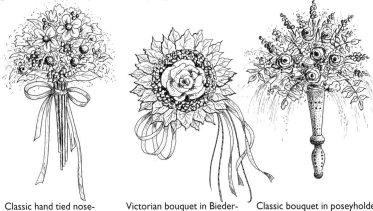

Classic hand tied nosegay, fragrant bouquet

Victorian bouquet in Biedermeier form in concentric rings

Classic bouquet in poseyholder, Victorian ball bouquet

Classical
Egyptians, some 2000 B.C., created extensive and magnificent gardens, and like us today, appreciated the beauty of nature. Foliage and flowers of *Cyperus papyrus* and Lotus Blossoms were revered and formed the basis of their bouquets.

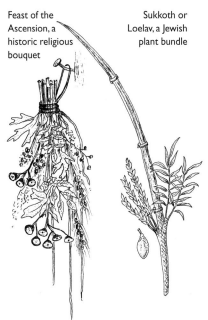

Feast of the Ascension, a historic religious bouquet

Sukkoth or Loelav, a Jewish plant bundle

During the reign of Elizabeth the First, nosegays became quite popular, and were carried daily to provide colour, fragrance and joy.

Today, however, we are more drawn to the opulent bouquets of Victorian times. Gardening was the rage in those times as it is now and it became fashionable to arrange romantic bouquets to carry or decorate the home. The nosegay or Tussie Mussie used as a 'Porte Bouquet' was carried in the hand or pinned to the gowns during the grand balls of the 19th century.

The full round Biedermeier bouquets also date from that period and are still as popular as ever.

Authentic classical bouquets can be made and interpreted by using the information pertaining to the period and style.

Bouquets for historical religious events
Memories of the past remind us of the religious festivals and customs, which were celebrated in medieval Europe and beyond, when for example, during the Feast of Ascension, wild flowers were gathered on August 15, and made into bouquets. These bouquets consisted of at least 7 different kinds of field flowers, herbs and fruits, and were blessed by the parish priest. The bouquets were then hung in the home, which according to legends, protected the home from evil spirits and violent storms.

Bouquets made of Boxwood were used during Palm Sunday.

The Jewish custom of using bouquets during the celebration of the Harvest Festival or Sukkoth, is to make a hand tied bouquet of the following: 1 palm leaf, 2 willow branches, 3 fragrant sprigs of myrtle and 1 lemon.

Bouquets interpreting Christian traditions and symbolisms can be developed by using a specific theme, e.g. a Biblical text or a quote from the Psalms. Base the choice of materials on these themes. General themes can be developed by using topics, such as: Peace, The Good Earth, Love, Healing, etc.

The above themes can be beautifully interpreted in floral combinations.

Contemporary
The 20th century displays a tremendous diversity in all forms of creative and visual expressions. Bouquets can form beautiful counterpoints which can blend or contrast with their graphic or bold forms and striking colour contrasts.

During the 1960's the linear floral style bouquet was introduced and much appreciated for its simplicity.

The waterfall bouquet or cascade dates from the late 19th century, and was at that time primarily used as a bridal bouquet. During the 1980's it became popular again, not only as a bridal bouquet, but also as an unique hand tied bouquet or vase arrangement.

Experimental
Every alternative form and technique belongs to the realm of experimental bouquets. For example, bound and tied construction techniques, braiding, gluing techniques, intertwining and weaving techniques form the basis of these types of designs.

The development and experimentation to seek new directions in bouquet making led to the creation of some new bouquet styles. It is a delightful challenge to give expression to technical know-how and creativity.

BOUQUET STYLES WITH VARIOUS OPTIONS

The function of the bouquet
There are numerous options and possibilities to create beautiful bouquets. It is impossible to discuss in great detail everything in this book. Much depends on the chosen binding techniques, but the creativity and our own inventiveness will play a large role in the total effect.
A bouquet is generally created for a specific function or purpose, and we select the flowers and form accordingly. The following bouquet forms are most popular:

The bunch
A bunch of flowers is not yet a bouquet. It is a collection of flowers of the same kind and stems cut at the same length.
The grower brings his flowers to the market in bunches of 5 to 30 stems, and are available as such at florists and supermarkets.

The fragrant bouquet
This is one of the simplest and most charming of bouquet styles. They are being made with a lovely variety of fragrant flowers, foliage, and/or aromatic herbs. The bouquet is arranged rather informally and has a simple round form. Stems are cut evenly after tying.

The vase bouquet
As the name implies, it is a bouquet tied in such a manner as to fit into a vase. Before doing so, stems must be recut.
There is a variety of bouquet styles from which to choose, but the all round form seems to be the most popular and fits in most areas in the home or office.

The sympathy bouquets
One sided tied bouquets are suitable as a funeral tribute or for a memorial service. The bouquet is usually placed flat and tied in such a way that the flowers and foliage stay in place. This is done by using short pieces of greens bent back to cover the stems of the bouquet. Ribbons are generally used as design elements and to provide a finishing touch.

Presentation bouquets
These bouquets are presented for special occasions. Different terminology is used by people in the trade which causes some confusion. It simply means that a bouquet has to reflect the occasion and purpose, and can, therefore, be created in all shapes and sizes.
A bouquet, which is presented on the podium of the theatre, should be quite large and showy. A bouquet, which is being presented during a T.V. program, a reception or for congratulatory purposes, can be quite large or small and delicate. There are many options: the choice depends on the occasion and the effect you wish to achieve.
We shall discuss a few possibilities:

◆ A showy bouquet for impact
As the title suggests, this bouquet must be large, impressive, and should make a great impact on the recipient. The bouquet can be made one sided or all round, and be of generous size.
◆ An easy to hold elegant bouquet
This bouquet is especially suitable for a presentation during a T.V. program, a reception, recital, etc. One can choose from an all round to a one sided bouquet. The style and form of the bouquet should be delicate and elegant. It may be finished with a fine quality ribbon.
◆ Reception or hand bouquet
Receptions are occasions which may require the presentation of a bouquet. These bouquets should be elegant, rather small and light weight, as well as properly balanced so they are easy to hold.

Almost any bouquet style is suitable to help celebrate the occasion, but it should be stressed to keep it on the small side.
◆ Bride's and bridesmaids' bouquets
The bride's bouquet or a small bouquet for the bridesmaids provide the ultimate challenge for creating a bouquet in the hand tied technique.
We suggest the parallel technique to ensure that the bundle of flower stems remain slender. Finish the stem bundle with ribbon, cording, banding or other appropriate material.
Suitable styles are the all round, symmetrical or asymmetrical, mixed or grouped, the waterfall or linear forms.
Alternate styles, in form and techniques are also excellent choices to create small works of floral art.
The bride's bouquet is an intimate bouquet of love, which should feast her eye, and enchant her with the beautifully chosen floral materials and exquisite finishing details. A moment and memory never to be forgotten!

BOUQUETS FOR SPECIAL OCCASIONS

Throughout the year, there are many occasions which call for a floral gift. We are always confronted with the same questions: what materials are suitable, how best to interpret a specific theme, idea or symbol, and what form, style or technique we should use.
A simple suggestion is to find out the specific reason for making a bouquet, whether for ourselves or a friend, and express a specific idea or theme for your bouquet. Follow your own feelings and 'capture the moment of the day'.
Rules for making bouquets are sometimes useful, but often, one should just ignore them.
Remember, the primary reason is to surprise your friends and loved ones with flowers.
A choice of floral suggestions is listed below. Add your own ideas to this list.

◆ St. Valentine's bouquet	◆ ....
◆ Mardi Gras	
◆ Easter	
◆ Secretaries' Day	◆ ....
◆ Mothers' Day	
◆ Fathers' Day	
◆ Christmas	◆ ....
◆ New Year's Eve	
◆ New Year's	
◆ Dried	◆ ....
◆ Theme	
◆ Symbolic	
◆ Exam	
◆ Horoscope	◆ ....
◆ Fragrant	
◆ Foliage	
◆ Seasonal	◆ ....
◆ Wild flower	
◆ Baby	
◆ Environmental	◆ ....
◆ Atmosphere	
◆ Herb	
◆ Apology	◆ ....
◆ Welcome	
◆ Children's	
◆ Exotic	◆ ....
◆ Friendship	
◆ Birthday	
◆ Thanksgiving	◆ ....

EXAMPLES OF HAND TIED BOUQUETS

Open (lacy) ajour form

ROUND AJOUR (LACY) BOUQUET

Symmetrical round and airy bouquets have been an all time favourite. They may be created in any colour combination, and when properly finished with foliage and ribbon, are a joy to behold.

In contrast with the more compact Biedermeier bouquet this bouquet is airy and round in shape and it is called 'Ajour', which means lacy in French. It is often called a Mille fleur, which is incorrect. Mille fleur means that we mix many varieties and colours together. The word Mille fleur does not suggest or indicate a bouquet style.

However, most round bouquets are now known as Mille fleur, which is derived from the Italian word Mille fiori, meaning 1000 flowers. The French word Mille fleur suggests many evenly distributed flowers. In both instances we use colourful combinations. It takes at least 25 flowers and foliage.

Opulent bouquets require a substantial number of blooms. The binding technique here is the sheaf or spiral technique (see pag 4).

Used are: *Tulipa. Alstroemeria, Myrica gale, Ruscus, Arachniodes adiantiformis, Leucothoe, Alnus, Thuja* and decorative touches of paper and foil.

ASYMMETRICAL ROUND FORM IN A MIXED COMPOSITION

The best known style of bouquets are the alround symmetrically tied bouquets. This form can be quite compact, or somewhat airy and loosely arranged. The round forms are generally known as the Biedermeier bouquets, which date from around 1820 - 1850. During this romantic period, flowers were arranged in a very compact manner and sometimes in a very decorative and geometric fashion. It takes as little as 25 stems to make an attractive small bouquet. However, a medium sized bouquet takes at least 40 stems or more, depending on the thickness of the stems, the shape and size of the flowers.

Tulips, Anemones or Ranunculus tend to 'grow' in water, and will, therefore, alter the shape of the bouquet in a few days, making the total effect lighter and more relaxed.

The tying technique used is spiral (see page 4).

Materials used are: *Alstroemeria, Veronica, Cytisus, Hypericum, Bouvardia, Ammi majus, Callistephus chinensis, Asparagus umbellatus, A. setaceus, Ruscus, Photinia* x *fraseri* 'Red Robin'.

Compact bouquet form

THE FRAGRANT BOUQUET

Flowers from the garden, the meadow or a fine assortment from the florist are all excellent choices for this informal and fragrant bouquet. It is fashioned in a round shape and has a graceful open character.

This lovely bouquet can be made with short stemmed flowers, e.g. 15 - 25 cm, tied together with assorted foliage. Herbs and/or fragrant flowers are key for this type of bouquet.

The tying technique is the spiral or sheaf (see page 4). Used are *Brunnera, Saponaria, Nepeta, Anemone* and *Hedera.*

Talking about fragrance

At last we are able to smell the flowers. Growers have taken the initiative and are growing fragrant varieties again. There are an abundance of fragrant flowers and herbs in the garden, and Roses especially are favourite.

Choose varieties which are compatible in fragrance.

The bouquet form is yours to decide, but the round form seems most acceptable.

Do not use too many fragrances together, as they may disturb the 'smell' effect. It is better to use a little bit here and there or concentrate on one fragrance.

Fun to make are tiny fragrant bunches or bouquets.

These can be included in the large bouquet, but separated between other flowers, so as not to confuse the individual fragrances.

Fragrances exhibit their own characteristics, for instance, sweet, spicy, fresh, woody, intoxicating, etc. Also remember, that fragrances can be heavy and irritating, especially to the sick, and people with allergies.

Fragrant bouquet, upright style

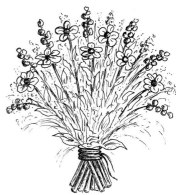

Fragrant bouquet, opulent style

ALL ROUND COMPACT FORM WITH GROUPED MATERIALS

A bouquet in a compact form, whereby the materials are used in a grouped fashion, gives rise to many creative expressions. The bouquet may be arranged in a symmetrical or asymmetrical form.

When the flowers are grouped, they appear more compact, giving the bouquet a solid look.

Position the individual small groups of flowers in the bouquet. Turn the bouquet in the hand until it has the desired shape and all small bunches are used. Tie cording or twine around the stems.

When selecting the small groups of material, pay special attention to colour, form and texture. A contemporary touch can be included in the bouquet by using vines, tufts of wool, spun fiberglass, and other unusual transparent materials, which can be pulled over or through the bouquet.

The binding technique is sheaf or spiral (see page 4).

Materials used are: *Gerbera, Limonium, Lysimachia, Thalictrum, Papaver, Paeonia, Campanula glomerata, Hydrangea, Hypericum, Erigeron, Cotinus, Hedera, Ruscus, Thuja occidentalis,* beargrass *(Xerophyllum tenax).*

Proper tufts are arranged under the flowers to provide a finishing touch.

ALL ROUND ASYMMETRICAL BOUQUET STYLE

Bouquets, which are made in an airy, lacy 'Ajour' style are easy to make, and exhibit a certain degree of elegance. The bouquet shown on this page is not compact and round, but uses small groups of material in different lengths, giving it a playful effect and is pleasing to look at from all sides.

If one uses larger groups of flowers, and increase the contrasting elements of colour and/or texture between them, the overall form and effect becomes more restful.

You will need at least 30 flowers and some foliage. A little more material makes it even more festive.

The binding technique is sheaf or spiral (see page 4).

Materials used are: *Brodiaea, Pulsatilla, Salvia, Veronica, Centaurea cyanus, Limonium, Eucalyptus, Asparagus umbellatus, Asparagus virgatus, Hosta.* The bouquet is placed in a glass vase.

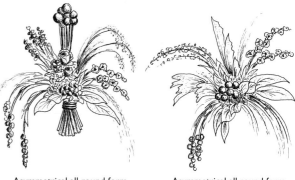

Asymmetrical all round form, frontal view

Asymmetrical all round form, top view

ONE SIDED MIXED BOUQUET

The classic one sided bouquet is not made as often as the all round bouquet. It is primarily used as a presentation or show bouquet, and can also be used as a sympathy or memorial bouquet. In the case of a sympathy bouquet, a slight adjustment should be made regarding the styling and ribbon treatment.

The one sided bouquet requires quite a bit of material due to the compact one sided form. It can be made, in either an acute symmetrical form or arranged in a more informal fashion.

With respect to colour, we can use a monochromatic, e.g. tone on tone, a polychromatic or multi colour scheme. The more colours are used, the brighter, bolder and more festive the bouquet becomes. The triangular bouquet is widest at the base. Binding technique used is the spiral or sheaf (see page 4-5).

Used are: *Rosa* 'Larinii', *Hypericum, Aconitum, Trachelium, Alstroemeria, Dianthus barbatus, Spiraea bumalda, Ruscus, Cotinus, Asparagus virgatus.*

a. One sided symmetrical bouquet, frontal view

b. One sided symmetrical bouquet, side view

c. One sided symmetrical bouquet, top view

BIEDERMEIER BOUQUET IN CONCENTRIC RINGS

Biedermeier bouquets have a half round symmetrical compact form, whereby all the materials used are placed in concentric circles. It is an old but always an unique and interesting bouquet form. When a contrasting colour combination is used and the bouquet is appropriately finished with ribbon, foliage or tule, it becomes a feast for the eye.

We make the bouquet in rings of different colour contrasts or use rings of large flowers contrasting with very small flowers or other material. The centre bloom should be large and is placed somewhat higher in the design. This bouquet form was very popular in the 19th century and was often used as a bridal bouquet. The binding technique is usually spiral, but for bridal bouquets the parallel technique is preferred. To make this bouquet, start as follows:

1. Take the centre flower in the hand.
2. Make a ring of flowers around the centre flower, making sure they are level and blooms are uniform in size.
3. Place rings of flowers in such a way that the bouquet takes on a dome or pyramid shape, depending on your preference.
4. Finish the bouquet with foliage, or tule and ribbon.

Used are: *Solidago, Hypericum, Achillea filipendulina, Echinops ritro, plume Hydrangea, Bergenia cordifolia,* ribbon.

Biedermeier in concentric rings, step by step

Biedermeier with tule and ribbon finishing touches

ONE SIDED GROUPED BOUQUET

A modern classic bouquet is made by the grouping of materials. The one sided bouquet is an Isosceles triangle, which has two sides of equal length. The form can be either acutely symmetrical, or made in a more relaxed fashion, as illustrated in the photo.

Group the materials to colour, kind or variety, and use them in such a way as to create a strong contrast.

The base of the bouquet is wider, and can be accentuated by adding more foliage. Having mastered this bouquet style, and by reducing the material in the bouquet, we are gradually leading up to a method or technique to create a playful and relaxed linear style bouquet.

Binding technique is the sheaf or spiral (see page 4).

Used are: *Nerine bowdenii, Leucadendron, Liatris, Dianthus* 'Sorentino', *Celosia* 'Sharon', *Mentha, Limonium* 'Emille', *Hypericum, Asparagus virgatus, Asparagus setaceus, Eucalyptus, Aspidistra elatior, Euonymus.*

Frontal view

Side view

Top view

LINEAR ALL ROUND BOUQUET

The all round linear bouquet is always popular. It has a spacious, playful appearance, and projects a spontaneous contemporary feeling. There should be lots of space between the materials, groups or single stems of flowers, which is characteristic of this type of bouquet.

The most interesting form is asymmetrical, which means that the bouquet is uneven in form. Sometimes a single branch projecting out of the bouquet creates a stunning effect. One does not need a great deal of material, but the right kinds are important, as are contrasting forms and good balance.

Use foliage which gives a restful appearance, for example, *Hedera, Aspidistra* or fern. This bouquet can be used for the same occasions as discussed in the one sided linear bouquet. The binding technique is sheaf or parallel (see page 4).

Used are: *Helianthus annuus, Asparagus setaceus, Aspidistra elatior.* Rolled copper wire is used to give a decorative effect.

LINEAR ONE SIDED BOUQUET

Playful lines, space and exciting form describe this bouquet style. The linear bouquet is made by providing lots of space between the materials. The voids thus obtained are necessary to create a counterpoise within the bouquet. Lines and voids are the hallmark of this bouquet style. By developing an asymmetrical form, and using strong groups of flowers and foliage, especially in the center, we are then able to create beautiful and elegant bouquets. The form is one sided, and can be used as a bridal bouquet, presentation bouquet, show bouquet, vase bouquet, and even a sympathy bouquet.

The binding technique used is parallel, but the spiral technique is often used (see page 4).

Materials used are: *Zantedeschia, Hydrangea, Vriesea, Skimmia japonica, Clematis, Sorghum durra, Celosia plumosa, Alchemilla mollis, Scabiosa seedpods, Buddleya, Araucaria, Fatsia, Asparagus densiflorus* 'Meyers', *Equisetum japonica, Hedera,* thyphaleaf, beargrass (*Xerophyllum tenax*).

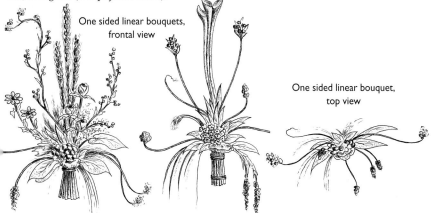

One sided linear bouquets, frontal view

One sided linear bouquet, top view

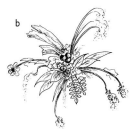

a. All round linear bouquet, frontal view
b. All round linear bouquet, top view

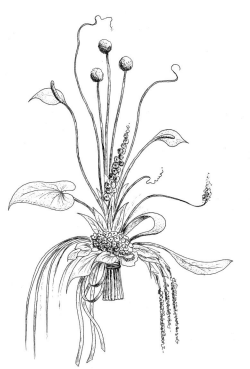

Large show bouquet, frontal view, linear style

SHOW BOUQUETS

These types of bouquets are primarily used as presentation bouquets for theatre performances and large receptions.

The purpose is to make the bouquet qua size and form suit the specific occasion, the space and preferably the colour of the recipient's clothing.

The bouquet should be visible from a reasonable distance.

It is also important to note the colour of the artificial light so that the flowers look well together. Dark colours, including deep reds and blue purple, recede in artificial light.

The presence of the bouquet is important, because, we not only want to honour the recipient, but also awe them with a magnificent bouquet.

We can group or mix the materials in the bouquet, and can fashion it in a symmetrical or asymmetrical style.

Ribbon is often important, because it reinforces the 'show' element.

Choose clear, fresh and soft colours for best effect, and use restful foliage for support.

Binding technique is sheaf or parallel (see page 4-5).

Used are: *Liatris, Gerbera, Dianthus caryophyllus, Alstroemeria, Erica, Genista, Freesia, Viburnum opulus* 'Roseum', *Ranunculus, Arachniodes adiantiformis*, Sword fern, *Aristolochia*, ribbon.

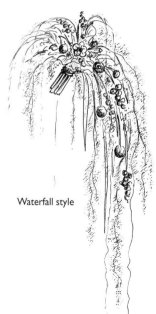

Waterfall style

THE WATERFALL OR CASCADE BOUQUET

The waterfall bouquet is a natural and spontaneous form, which creates an impression of elegance, volume and spaciousness. It projects a certain radiation.

The bouquet has a wide variety of uses, including bridal bouquets, presentation or vase bouquets.

A cascade suggests a waterfall, which implies that all materials are arranged in a downward 'cascading' fashion. A little space between the material is advisable to prevent a stunted look. The bouquet can be created with just a few vines, tendrils, flowers and foliage, or an abundance of material depending on your choice.

It is usually asymmetrical in form, but a symmetrical bouquet can be interesting, albeit somewhat staid. The material you select will depend on the chosen design. Flowers and foliage can either contrast or be very harmonious pertaining to the form and structure. Ribbon, woolen threads, cord, twine and long tendrils tend to create a cascading effect, and indeed reinforce it.

Binding technique is usually sheaf or spiral (see page 4-5).

Used are: *Limonium, Ammi majus, Astilbe, Dicentra spectabilis, Spiraea, Paeonia, Eucalyptus, Asparagus setaceus*, tendrils of *Polygonum aubertii* and ribbon.

17

BRIDAL BOUQUETS, THE MOST IMPORTANT OF ALL

The hand tied technique lends itself to creative bridal bouquets. A few beautiful flowers such as *Calla* lily with foliage and ribbon can be developed into a beautiful arm bouquet. A linear bouquet, a cascade or structure bouquet, or an all round tied bouquet in various styles are also a few of the possibilities.

The most used, however, is the Biedermeier form.

It is important, that the bouquet is lightweight and easily carried. If necessary, part of the material can be wired, so that the stem can be bent. Ideally, stems which are curved naturally are preferred, but not always available. Tie ribbon around the bundle of stems as a finishing touch. Provide other details if desired to make this bouquet of love the most beautiful of all bouquets.

Used are: *Anthurium, Hydrangea, Setaria, Ageratum houstonianum, Gerbera* 'Ballet', *Asparagus setaceus, Eucalyptus, Hedera, Thypa* foliage, Beargrass (*Xerophyllum tenax*), and decorative materials.

The bridesmaid's bouquet, large or small, is made in the same hand tied technique as the bride's bouquet. It can be simply made from a few small flowers and foliage.

The most popular style is all round (Biedermeier).

Finish the bouquet with a collar of foliage or tule around the base of the bouquet with a bow tied around the stems, and voila... a charming bouquet is born. See 'cradle' bouquet which is made in the same manner (see page 19).

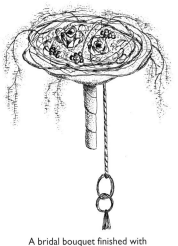

A bridal bouquet finished with
ribbon and cording

Three different styles of hand tied bridal bouquets

BALL BOUQUET

A ball bouquet was very fashionable in the 19th century. Unfortunately, this type of bouquet is seldom made today. Nevertheless, it would be a nice gesture to surprise a lady before the dance with a delicate and elegant bouquet.

The bouquet should be small, well constructed, and featherlight. Use durable flowers with a delightful fragrance. The preferred style is the all round form like a Biedermeier, mixed, grouped, or with rings of flowers of various forms and colours. The cascade styling was popular during the last part of the 19th century.

Fasten a ribbon loop to the bouquet, so that it can be worn or carried on the wrist during the dance. Sometimes, a ring is attached, so that the thumb can be inserted.

The bouquet should be finished neatly and conceal all wires. Glue is used on occasion with excellent results.

Binding technique is parallel (see page 5).

Used are: *Gerbera, Limonium, Campanula glomerata, Alchemilla mollis, Asparagus umbellatus*, ribbon.

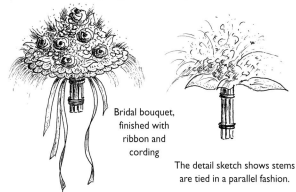

Bridal bouquet, finished with ribbon and cording

The detail sketch shows stems are tied in a parallel fashion.

CRADLE BOUQUET

It is indeed very charming and attentive to surprise mother and baby with a delicate bouquet, which can be hung from the baby's crib or cradle. It is the very first bouquet that is being presented to the newborn, and hopefully will be followed by many more.

It is important, that the flowers used are not too fragrant, allergy causing or subject to shedding. The bouquet should be small, dainty and round.

For girls, soft pink toned bouquets are the tradition, and for boys, a blue toned combination is the norm. A festive, mixed combination is a nice alternative.

To increase the longevity of the bouquet, wrap the stems in wet tissue, and put in a plastic bag. Cover bag with ribbon, and finish with a bow.

Parallel is the preferred binding technique (see page 5).

Used are: *Rosa* 'Pink Tango', *Gypsophila, Erica, Hydrangea, Chamaecyparis pisifera* 'Boulevard'.

Decorative finishing touches: irridescent foil and ribbon.

Charming cradle bouquets

TEXTURE - STRUCTURE BOUQUET

This type of bouquet is becoming very popular because it is suitable for many occasions. Contrasting materials in various textures are combined to create a bouquet which has great appeal and very unique characteristics.

The best way to make this bouquet is to group the materials as to variety, kind and colour. It is important to provide strong contrasts between the groups to heighten the effect.

The compact half round form, similar to the Biedermeier bouquet, is the preferred style for this texture bouquet.

The elements of texture and structure can lead to a very unique bridal bouquet.

The bouquet can be hand tied, and combined with gluing and wiring techniques.

Binding techniques can be varied, depending on choice.

Used are: *Rosa, Hydrangea macrophylla, Amaranthus hypichondriacus, Skimmia, Setaria, Thymus vulgaris, Mentha, Hedera, Asparagus umberllatus, Aspidistra, Thuja occidentalis, Taxus baccata* 'Fastigiata', Beargrass (*Xerophyllum tenax*), fabric, and small bundles of cinnamon sticks bound with copper wire.

Examples of structure bouquets

A LATTICE SUPPORT STRUCTURE

Lattice or grid support construction and branch structures are an interesting development in bouquet making. The bouquet will take on a different look, which is rather interesting and appealing.

We use twigs to make a grid construction, and fasten 4 florist wires at each side, which will become part of the bouquet handle. You can also use twigs instead. The twigs in the grid are tied with raffia, twine or wire. Arrange the flowers and greens through the openings of the branch construction as well as underneath. Cascading materials should drape over the construction for support, while a few materials, placed below, add interest.

Arrange the flowers in a free and spontaneous fashion, so the bouquet does not look too structured. Tie the stems of the bouquet with cording, twine, ribbon and other decorative materials.

Used are: *Gloriosa, Ranunculus, Veronica, Amaranthus caudatus, Asparagus setaceus, Pittosporum, Euphorbia, Aspidistra elatior*, Beargrass (*Xerophyllum tenax*).

The grid is constructed of the branches of *Cornus alba* 'Sibirica', and is tied with raffia.

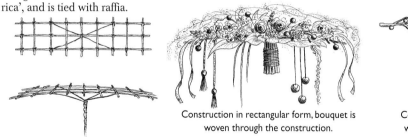

Construction in rectangular form, bouquet is woven through the construction.

Construction with handle

WREATH BRANCH STRUCTURE AS A BASIS OF ARRANGING

Unusual bouquets may be created by using a round construction of branch material as the basis of a bouquet. Willow branches are used to fashion a wreath of approximately 35 cm in diameter; the ends tied together with twine or raffia. Four florist wires are fastened equidistant around the wreath, which will form the handle of the bouquet. Twigs will do as well.

Arranging is as follows: Hold the wreath in the hand by the wires, and arrange all flowers and foliage in, over and under the wreath structure.

The bouquet is finished in the usual manner.

The material choice is wide open, and colours used can be either restrained or dynamic.

The binding technique can be either sheaf or parallel (see page 4-5).

Used are: *Nerine, Rosa, Limonium, Erica, Amaranthus hypochondriacus, Asparagus setaceus, Asparagus densiflorus* 'Meyers', *Eucalyptus*.

The basic wreath construction is made from *Salix matsudana* 'Tortuosa' (Cork screw willow) and tied with raffia.

Sphere/round construction

TIP: IN CASE YOU DO NOT HAVE BRANCH MATERIAL, IT IS POSSIBLE TO SUBSTITUTE SMALL PREMADE HAY, STRAW OR GRAPE VINE WREATHS, WHICH ARE COMMERCIALLY AVAILABLE.

A TRIANGLE OR ELLIPSE BRANCH CONSTRUCTION AS A BASE OF ARRANGING

In this technique we use branches to form an asymmetrical triangular grid pattern. Four heavy wires are fastened around the triangle and become the handle for this bouquet. Do not make the triangle too large or heavy in case it slips out of the bouquet. Hold the wires in the hand, so that the triangle structure is horizontal. Place all floral material between and under the construction in the bouquet.

Select interesting cascading material, which can drape over and spill out of the bouquet. The whole bouquet should exhibit a playful effect with part of the structure showing.

Used are: *Gerbera, Tulipa, Ammi majus, Ixora, Ogiopogon, Asparagus setaceus, Ruscus, Amaranthus, Solidago.*

The asymmetrical construction was made with *Salix matsudana* 'Tortuosa', and tied together with twine.

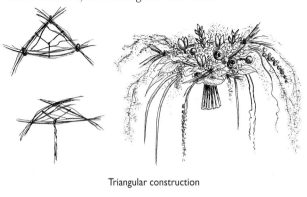

Triangular construction

Ellipse shaped construction

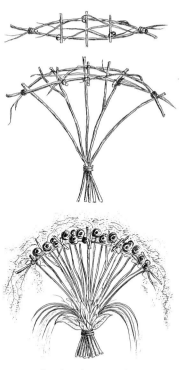

Fan shaped construction

FANSHAPED BRANCH CONSTRUCTION AS A BASIS

This unusual two sided fan bouquet is created by using 2 long branches to which small pieces of twigs are fastened, resembling a railroad track.

Heavy wire is used to pull the ends inward in order to create a fan or dome shape. Wires become part of the handle of the bouquet.

Place all flowers and foliage in the branch structure in a casual, unstudied manner. Cover underside with some foliage, but be sure to leave part of the structure exposed.

Branch construction techniques, described in the last four bouquets, can also be very effective, when used in a hand tied bridal bouquet.

Binding technique sheaf or parallel (see page 4-5).

Used are: *Papaver nudicaule, Asparagus setaceus, Aspidistra elatior, Ruscus.*

The dome shaped basis construction is made from *Cornus alba* 'Sibirica'.

DRIED BOUQUETS

Dried and silk (fabric) flowers are excellent choices for making hand tied bouquets.

A combination of a basis form, to which other materials are added and glued, is another option.

Delicate dried flowers should be made into small bundles, tied with string or tape, before being added to the bouquet. Dried flowers are available in a wide assortment, but you are also able to dry them yourself, and use them during the winter to make lovely bouquets. The drying of flowers is a very enjoyable hobby.

The binding technique could be a parallel or sheaf (see page 4-5).

Given the enormous selection of dried flowers available, and/or your own dried materials, it should be fairly easy to choose the right kind to create a beautiful and long lasting bouquet; one which complements and enhances your home interior.

HOROSCOPE BOUQUET

A birthday, or a birth, provides us with an excellent opportunity to create a bouquet, which interprets a person's horoscope.

Use the colour of flowers, associated with the particular sign of the Zodiac, and add, if you wish, an accessory to accentuate the idea or theme.

The style of the bouquet is of one's own choice, but the round bouquet seems the preferred style.

There are special ribbons, as well as enclosure cards, depicting the various astrological signs.

There are 12 signs of the Zodiac.

The German born astrologer Ruth Zucker has assembled a series of colours associated with these signs.

One can make the bouquet in the specific period of time or from a different era altogether. The availability of flowers and colours will in fact determine your choice.

PISCES *(Feb. 19 - March 20)*
Combination of soft colours, e.g. lilac, blue and pink

ARIES *(March 21 - April 19)*
Thorny branches, warm reds and yellow colours

TAURUS *(April 20 - May 20)*
Bright summer bouquets

GEMINI *(May 21 - June 21)*
Blue and yellow, with a green dividing line in the centre

CANCER *(June 22 - July 22)*
Pink, dark blue, white, turquoise and beige

LEO *(July 23 - August 22)*
Yellow and orange

VIRGO *(August 23 - September 22)*
White, with greens, if desired

LIBRA *(September 23 - October 23)*
Yellow, blue and white

SCORPIO *(October 24 - November 21)*
Strong colours in blue, red and purple, including something thorny

SAGITTARIUS *(November 22 - December 21)*
Red, rust and yellow gold

CAPRICORN *(December 22 - January 19)*
Dark blue, white and red

AQUARIUS *(January 20 - February 18)*
Combination of either violet, or blue with yellow, orange or pink

Binding technique is sheaf (see page 4).

The bouquet pictured is for a Libra and consists of *Dendranthema* 'Napoli', *Gerbera, Rosa* 'Noblesse', *Solidago, Amaranthus caudatus, Lysimachia vulgaris, Carthamus tinctorius, Veronica, Hydrangea, Weigelia, Setaria, Eucalyptus, Leucothoe.* The ribbon and enclosure card complete the symbolic gesture.

TIP: YOU CAN PRESENT A HOROSCOPE BOUQUET THROUGHOUT THE YEAR; THE FLOWER CHOICE DEPENDS ON THE SEASON.

AUTUMN BOUQUET

Autumnal bouquets express the beauty of the season. Each season has its own atmosphere. Spring is tender and full of expectation, of new life and growth. The summer displays an abundance of colour, fragrance and richness. The autumn exudes warm tints and tones, is romantic and provides us with a bountiful harvest of the earlier seasons. The winter is calm and suggests quiet and peace, but displays unexpected moments of small discoveries in flowering species as well as the green and brown nuances of shrubs and evergreens.
The countries near the equator usually experience wet and dry seasons of the year. Look for a combination to depict a particular season, and create your own bouquet full of romance, atmosphere and charm. Themes, such as: Spring Melody, Summer Dream, Autumn Song or Winter Mood are some of the suggestions.
This bouquet gives an interpretation of autumn, but many variations are possible.
The binding technique is the sheaf or parallel (see page 4-5).
Used in this bouquet are the following: *Hydrangea, Dendranthema, Pennisetum, Craspedia globosa, Spiraea bumalda, Ligustrum vulgaris, Rudbeckia nitida, Weigelia.*

FOLIAGE BOUQUET

It is possible to create an exciting bouquet with foliage of any size, shape or form. Enjoy and discover the beauty of the large variety of foliage and the numerous nuances of green, grey, yellow, red, pink, blue and other tints in which foliage appears. Nature is indeed beautiful!
Bring an ode to foliage by creating a magnificent composition entitled: 'Green is beautiful', sensual and challenging.
Add to your bouquets spent inforescence, seed pods, etc. to create an extra dimension.
The binding technique chosen for this bouquet is the sheaf method (see page 4).
Used are: *Thalictrum, Papaver, Viburnum* berries, *Bergenia cordifolia, Hedera, Buxus sempervirens, Chamaecyparis obtusa* 'Nana Gracilis', *Thuja occidentalis, Iris seedpods, Rosmarinus, Polygonum aubertii.*
The bouquet is placed in a large Ecri vase.

WILDFLOWER OR FIELD BOUQUET

Flowers picked in the meadows, the roadside or some obscure corner in the neighbourhood, offer unlimited opportunities to make beautiful and 'natural' looking bouquets. Remember, that certain species of wild flowers do not last long in water, and are therefore better left in the field for others to enjoy. Some provinces and states prohibit the picking of certain flowers by law, because they are on the endangered species list. The months of May, June and July are ideal times to pick and create large bouquets of field flowers, consisting of grasses, buttercups, poppies, cornflower and many other species. Binding technique is the sheaf method (see page 4).

Used in this bouquet are: Sorrel, Daisies, Buttercups, Queen Anne's lace, Clover, Rapeseed, Chamomile.The bouquet is placed in an antique jar.

EASTER BOUQUET

Easter, the feast of spring, as well as the resurrection of the Lord, is a special feast. The atmosphere is spring, the budding of trees, new life, growth and hope. These feelings should be expressed in the bouquet. The colours of this season are predominantly yellow, green, white and pink, and should preferably be made up with spring flowers and budding branches. Easter elements, for example eggs, feathers, birdnests, Easter chicks etc., can be part of the bouquet.

The binding technique is the sheaf or parallel method (see page 4-5).

Used are the following: *Viburnum opulus* 'Roseum', *Cytisus, Ranunculus, Tulipa* 'Yokohama', *Buxus sempervirens, Gaultheria salal, Thuja, Myrica gale.* The basis of the bouquet is a woven nest of willow branches.

MOTHER'S DAY

Mother's Day is the ideal day to give flowers. Bouquets are part of this day, and come in all possible combinations. One can create a heart shape which can form the centre of the bouquet. A simple technique is to place small hearts between the flowers in the bouquet or glue them on the leaves. Another idea is to fashion a heart out of willow branches or wire, and use it in a linear style bouquet. This combination is very effective. Irrespective of the style used, the bouquet should be spectacular. Alternatively, one can think in terms of a lovely bouquet for children, which they can present to Mom on her special day. Flowers should be delicate, sweet and affordable. Binding technique is the sheaf or parallel (see page 4-5). Flowers used are: *Dendranthema, Lilium, Dianthus caryophyllus, Limonium, Ammi majus, Hypericum, Asparagus virgatus, Ruscus, Arachniodes adiantiformis, Taxus baccata* 'Fastigiata', including decorative materials, such as Dekofaser, acrylic fabric and bullion, which provide strong accent and ambiance to this opulent looking bouquet.

Mother's Day bouquet
with a heart shape

CHRISTMAS BOUQUET

Christmas is one of the most celebrated feasts in the Christian world. The atmosphere reflects the richness of the season, the joy and remembrance of the birth of Jesus. The bouquets should be an expression of these emotions. Winter greens are favourite, e.g. conifers of all kinds, holly and pine cones, but also the colours of flowers and accessories associated with this season, for example, red and white, gold and silvertian.
A Christmas bouquet does not need to be traditional to be

effective, but should nevertheless convey the spirit and ambiance of the season. The binding technique of this bouquet is the sheaf method (see page 4-5).
Used are the following: *Chamaecyparis obtusa* 'Nana Gracilis', *Cham. lawsoniana* 'Stewartii', *Cham. pisifera* 'Boulevard', *Cham. pisifera* 'Plumosa Aurea', *Pinus* 'Mugo Mugo', *Pinus strobus, Hedera, Hydrangea, Prunus laurocerasus* 'Zabeliana', *Ilex*, pine cones and *Punica granatum.* Decorative features included in the bouquet are: Lamé, ribbon, cording, gold bullion and gold stars.

CREATIVE EXPERIMENTAL BOUQUETS

Who does not yearn the freedom to do, what we really want to do? The idea is that we try to develop a concept or design which has not been done before, free of rules and regulations. Something original! You can experiment with binding techniques, or the way in which you arrange the stems, etc.
Before you start, it may be wise to review the styles and techniques you have learned. See if you can improve on the techniques, composition, colour combinations, and finishing touches. Tempt yourself to a journey of discovering experimental forms, styles and techniques. There are many more options and possibilities regarding bouquet making.
The binding technique is your choice: sheaf, parallel or alternative methods (see page 4-5).
Used in this composition are: *Limonium* 'Saint Pierre', *Amaranthus caudatus, Hypericum, Aconitum, Rosa, Euonymus, Echinops ritro, Deutzia, Salix matsudana* 'Tortuosa', *Eryngium planum, Cotinus, Saponaria (Vaccaria hispanica), Hedera*, tendrils of *Polygonum aubertii*. Basis of this bouquet is a small straw wreath. The flowers are arranged through and under the wreath form of which part is exposed.

Idea for a creative variation

Creative bouquet in parallel technique

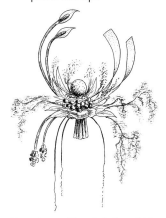

Linear bouquet in a circle (wreath) form

31

GLOSSARY OF BOTANICAL AND COMMON NAMES

A

Achillea	Yarrow
Aconitum	Monkshood
Ageratum	Floss flower
Alchemilla	Lady's mantle
Alstroemeria	Peruvian Lily
Amaranthus	Love-lies-bleeding
Ammi majus	Lace flower
Anemone	Windflower
Anthurium	Anthurium
Arachniodes	Leather fern
Araucaria	Monkey puzzle
Aristolochia	Birth wort
Asparagus	Asparagus

B

Bergenia	Bergenia
Bouvardia	Bouvardia
Brodiaea	Triteleia
Brunnera	Siberian bugloss
Buddleya	Butterfly bush
Buxus	Boxwood

C

Callistephus	China aster
Campanula	Bell flower
Celosia	Cocks comb
Centaurea	Corn flower, Bachelor's button
Chamaecyparis pisifera	False cypress
Clematis	Clematis
Cotinus	Smoke tree
Craspedia	Drumstick
Cytisus	Scotch broom

D

Dendranthema	Chrysanthemum
Dianthus barbatus	Sweet William
Dianthus caryophillus	Carnation
Dicentra	Bleeding heart

E

Echinops	Globe thistle
Equisitum	Horse tail
Erica	Heather
Erigeron	Flea bane
Eryngium	Sea holly
Eucalyptus	Eucalyptus
Euonymus	Euonymus
Euphorbia	Spurge

F

Fatsia	Castor oil plant
Freesia	Freesia

G

Gaulteria	Salal, Winter-green
Genista	Broom
Gerbera	Transvaal daisy
Gloriosa	Gloriosa Lily
Gypsophila	Baby's breath

H

Hedera	Ivy
Helianthus annuus	Sunflower
Hosta	Funkia
Hydrangea	Hydrangea
Hypericum	St. John's wort

I

Ilex	Holly
Ixora	Ixora

L

Leucothoe	Fetter bush
Liatris	Gay feather
Ligustrum	Privet
Limonium	Sea lavender
Lysimachia	Goose neck, Loose strife

M

Mentha	Mint
Myrica	Bayberry

N

Nepeta	Nepeta
Nerine	Guernsey lily

O

Ogiopogon	Ogiopogon

P

Paeonia	Peony
Papaver	Poppy
Pennisetum	Fountain grass
Photinia	Christmas berry
Pinus	Pine
Pittosporum	Pittosporum
Polygonum aubertii	Silver lace vine
Prunus	Flowering cherry, almond
Pulsatilla	Pasque flower
Punica	Pomegranate

R

Ranunculus	Ranunculus
Rudbeckia	Corn flower, Black eyed susan, Gloriosa daisies
Ruscus	Ruscus

S

Salix m. 'Tortuosa'	Corkscrew willow
Salvia	Sage
Saponaria	Soapwort
Scabiosa	Pincushion flower
Setaria	Setaria
Skimmia	Skimmia
Solidago	Golden rod
Spiraea	Astilbe

T

Taxus baccata	Yew
Thalictrum	Meadow rue
Thuja	Arborvitae, Cedar
Thymus	Thyme
Typha foliage	Bull rush

V

Veronica	Speedwell
Viburnum opulus	Snowball

W

Weigelia	Weigelia

X

Xerophyllum tenax	Bear grass

Z

Zantedeschia	Calla, Arum lily

For information regarding courses in Floral Design by Aad van Uffelen:
Holland College,
Chrysant 1,
2678 PA De Lier, The Netherlands,
tel. +31-174-513321.

A special thank you to all who have contributed to this book. Flowers for this book were supplied by Dutch flower wholesalers and exporters.

ISBN 90-6255-763-5
© 1997 Terra Publishing, Warnsveld
Photography: Jan van der Loos, Maasland, p. 11, 16, 18, 20, 24 and front cover
Sudipa, Taiwan, p. 15 (right) and 23 (above)
All other pictures: Aad van Uffelen

Lay-out: Nicolette Barenbrug, Haarlem
Printed by Tesink b.v., Zutphen